30 YEARS of Bo

M

Scrapbook Memories of a Michigan Football Icon

Edited by Francis J. Fitzgerald

TRIUMPH BOOKS

All photos in this book are reprinted from the University of Michigan Athletic Department archives.

Copyright ©1999 by Epic Sports.
All rights reserved.

ISBN 1-57243-382-5

No part of this work covered by the copyright hereon may be reproduced or used in any form or by any means graphic, electronic or mechanical, including photographing, recording, taping, or in electronic storage and retrieval systems without the permission of the publisher.

*Royalties from the sale of this book will be donated to
The Millie Schembechler Fund for Adrenal Cancer Research.*

Edited and compiled by: Epic Sports, Birmingham, AL
All rights and permissions obtained by: Epic Sports, Birmingham, AL

Bo Made Michigan a Winner Again

He arrived in Ann Arbor thirty years ago from Ohio, where he had coached the Miami University of Ohio football eleven for six seasons.

He was a man on a mission. A man in a hurry to return Michigan Wolverines football back to the big time, back to the glory that Fielding Yost and Fritz Crisler had delivered, back to an era when Michigan dominated the Big Ten.

Glenn Edward (Bo) Schembechler was 5-foot-10 and 185 pounds of pure determination. And his impact on the Wolverines' football future would be significant.

Prior to his arrival, the proud Michigan program had struggled. The Wolverines had won only one Big Ten football title in the previous eighteen seasons and had only five winning teams in the past ten seasons. And the Big House, that wonderful gridiron showplace that Yost had built, was averaging only 70,000 on autumn Saturdays — more than 30,000 under capacity.

Their locker room in Yost Fieldhouse was merely a room with nails on the wall and folding chairs.

Schembechler told his staff, who had traveled with him from Miami, "Men, we are going to make a few changes here." And he did.

On the first day of spring practice, he told his squad, "Now listen to me. All of you. I do not care if you are white or black or Irish or Italian or Catholic or Jewish or liberal or conservative. From this point on, I will treat you all the same — like dogs."

And he did. The Wolverines went through hell that first spring. Double sessions every day. Weight room workouts and extra running after practice. Extra running on Saturday.

Introduction

Bo was all over the place at those first practices — yelling, grabbing face masks, throwing players around, slapping them with his infamous yardsticks, demanding that each player give more of themselves, demanding that they get tougher.

Years later, Schembechler would recall, "That was exactly what they were looking for. Oh, they hated me. But when they saw the results, they felt better about themselves and accepted it."

During the middle of that memorable first spring practice, Schembechler hung up a sign in the Michigan football locker room. It read: "Those Who Stay Will Be Champions."

It would be their mantra.

The Wolverines started spring practice in March 1969 with 150 players but finished up with only 75 or 80.

But those who stayed were special. And they would be winners.

They opened the 1969 season by waxing Vanderbilt, 42-14, in front of 70,183. The same Vandy squad defeated Bear Bryant's Alabama team three weeks later, 14-10.

The next week, Bo's boys pounded Washington, 45-7. Only 49,684 Wolverine fans were at Michigan Stadium that afternoon.

After a 40-17 loss to Dan Devine's Missouri squad, Michigan entered the Big Ten schedule.

The Wolverines beat Purdue, 31-20, then stumbled against Michigan State, 23-12. But the steamroller was just getting warmed up.

Michigan ran over Minnesota, Wisconsin, Illinois, and Iowa the next four Saturdays.

Then came the big showdown with arch rival Ohio State. The Buckeyes had beaten Michigan in twelve of their previous eighteen meetings.

But Bo was determined to change this.

"When we came to Michigan, we set one goal," Bo explained. "And that was to beat Ohio State. Everything we did was done with that goal in mind.

Bo Made Michigan a Winner Again

"The Buckeyes were the No. 1 team in the country with twenty-two straight wins and had been named national champions the previous year (in 1968). They had won the Rose Bowl. Nobody could stop them.

"We designed our offense so that our defense could practice stopping it each day in practice. Beating Ohio State became our obsession."

When they finally met on November 22 in Ann Arbor, the Wolverines were seventeen-point underdogs.

The day of the game, when Michigan went out onto the field for pregame warmups in front of a packed crowd of 103,588, Schembechler saw that the Buckeyes were practicing on their side of the field.

Wasting no time, Schembechler walked up to Woody Hayes, his former coach at Miami of Ohio and for whom he had worked at Ohio State, and told him, "Coach, you are warming up on the wrong side of the field."

Woody fussed and cussed a bit. Then he moved.

The Michigan squad went wild after seeing Woody back down.

That afternoon, the Wolverines shocked the college football world with a 24-12 win over Ohio State. The victory gave Michigan the Big Ten title and a New Year's Day date with USC in the Rose Bowl.

It was only the beginning of good things to come.

In twenty-one seasons, Bo and company would rack up thirteen Big Ten titles and play in seventeen bowl games (including ten Rose Bowls). Seventeen times they finished in the top ten. He would post a record of 194-48-5 at Michigan with an overall record of 234-65-8 in twenty-seven seasons at Miami of Ohio and Michigan. During the 1970s, his Wolverines put together a 96-10-3 regular season record that was the best in college football.

When Bo retired after the 1989 season, he was the winningest active coach in the country and fifth on the all-time list — behind Paul (Bear) Bryant, Glenn (Pop) Warner, Amos Alonzo Stagg, and Woody Hayes.

He never had a losing season as a coach.

U-M athletic director Don Canham (middle) announces Bo's hiring to replace the retiring Bump Elliott (right) as Michigan's new head coach on Dec. 27, 1968.

Bo on the sidelines with Frank Titas during his first game at Michigan against Vanderbilt in 1969.

Bo and All-American tackle Dan Dierdorf inspect the special shoes that the Wolverines would wear on the new artificial turf in 1969.

When it came to dealing with officials, Bo was never shy in voicing his opinion.

Bo and an assistant coach review game films on a new film projector system.

On the sidelines of the game, Bo was at his best.

A reunion of Michigan's coaches prior to the 1969 Ohio State game: (left to right) Harry Kipke, Fritz Crisler, Bennie Oosterbaan, Bump Elliott and Bo.

Bo's win over Ohio State in 1969 will always be unforgettable with Wolverine fans.

Meeting with the press after the 1969 Ohio State game, Bo finally began to savor the win.

Bo at practice prior to the 1970 Rose Bowl game against Southern Cal.

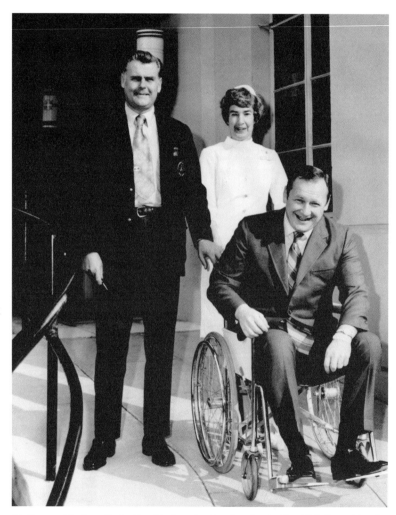

Bo leaves the hospital after his heart attack prior to the 1970 Rose Bowl.

Bo racked up a record of 194 wins, 48 losses and 5 ties at Michigan.

Tight end Jim Mandich and Bo discuss strategy in 1969.

Bo with his yardstick at practice. These were often helpful in getting a player's attention.

President Gerald Ford visits practice at Michigan in 1976.

Bo and All-American quarterback Rick Leach at a press conference prior to the 1977 Rose Bowl.

Bo erupts on the sideline against Ohio State in 1973.

Bo — the teacher — at practice in Ann Arbor in 1975.

After the Wolverines defeated Washington in the 1981 Rose Bowl, Bo led the celebration.

Bo with UCLA coach Terry Donahue prior to the 1983 Rose Bowl.

Bo and Auburn coach Pat Dye enjoy a cup of cajun coffee prior to the 1984 Sugar Bowl.

Bo and Iowa coach Hayden Fry before their epic match in 1985.

Bo and Penn State coach Joe Paterno testified before the Senate Judiciary Committee in 1983.

Bo and his All-American quarterback Jim Harbaugh on the sidelines in 1986.

Actor Pat O'Brien, who played Knute Rockne in the movie, Knute Rockne: All-American, and Bo at the 1977 Rose Bowl luncheon.

1980 Michigan-Notre Dame game program.

Bo's snarls often did more to motivate a player than a pep talk.

Bo consoles Michigan State coach George Perles after defeating the Spartans in 1988.

Bo, wearing his headphones, was a familiar sight on the sidelines in the 1970's and 1980's.

Bo instructs backup quarterback Christopher Zurbrugg on the sidelines in 1986.

A trio of Wolverine coaches: (left to right) Bump Elliott, Bo and Gary Moeller.

Bo and Notre Dame coach Lou Holtz after the Wolverines' win in 1986.

Bo in disappointment on the sidelines during the difficult 1984 season.

Bo at his weekly press conference at the Weber's Inn in Ann Arbor.

President Gerald Ford (left), Wolverines basketball coach Johnny Orr (right) and Bo compare scores after a golf match in 1986.

Bo voices his displeasure at an official's call.

Bob Hope (left), Rose Bowl queen Yasmine Delavari and Bo pose for the photographers prior to the 1990 Rose Bowl.

Bo was a coach with many emotions and had many unique ways of getting his message across.

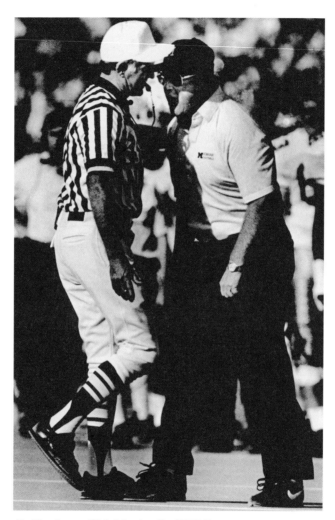

Bo blasts an official during the 1989 Iowa game.

Notre Dame end Dean Masztak meets Bo in 1981.

Indiana basketball coach Bobby Knight enjoys a moment of laughter with his old friend, Bo, in 1988.

Bo adjusts his tie before meeting the press at the 1989 Rose Bowl.

U-M president James Duderstadt (middle) and President Gerald Ford (right) view a model of Schembechler Hall with Bo in 1988.

Bo and his top offensive assistant Gary Moeller (right) on the sidelines against Ohio State in 1987.

Minnie Mouse greets Bo at Disneyland during a Rose Bowl visit in the 1980's.

TV broadcaster Lindsey Nelson (middle) listens to Bo at a Big Ten dinner in Chicago in 1987.

Bo flings a pass to the press before the Wolverines' bowl game with BYU in 1984.

Bo with U-M basketball coach Steve Fisher after the Wolverines won the NCAA title in 1989.

Bo considered it a good practice if he only broke 3 yardsticks at practice.

Bo with the 1989 Associated Press national championship trophy.

Bo listens to his assistants on the sideline in 1986.

David Letterman was amazed when listening to Bo's tales.

Bo makes a point with the press.

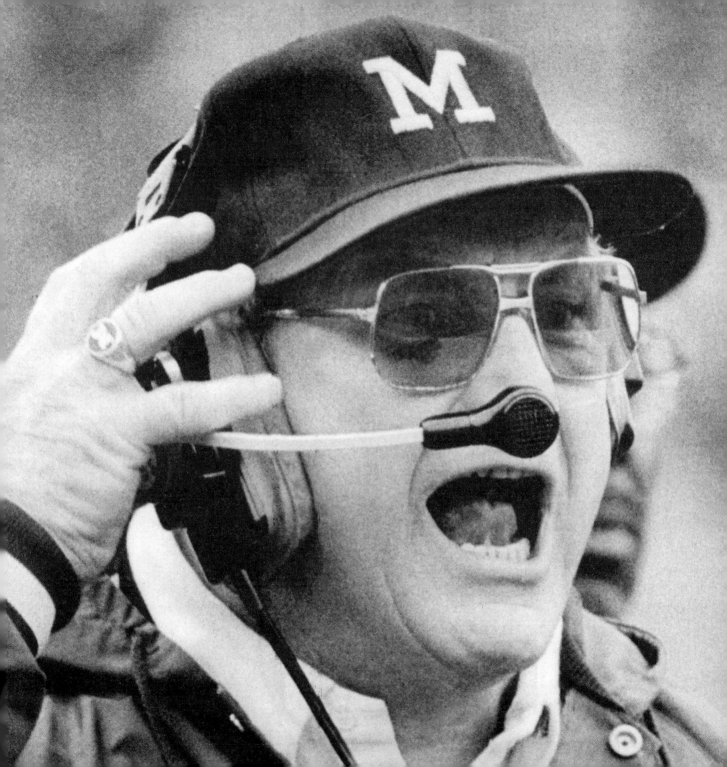

Bo relaxes after his final game in the 1990 Rose Bowl.

Bo on the mound at Tiger Stadium after becoming president of the Tigers in January 1990.

Bo and Detroit Tigers manager Sparky Anderson at spring training in 1990.

This Bo-wannabe turned up at a Detroit Pistons basketball game in 1990.

Much of Bo's time with the Tigers was spent in public relations work to get a new stadium built.

The Tigers braintrust: owner Tom Monaghan, Sparky Anderson and Bo.

Bo served as president of the Detroit Tigers for three seasons in 1990-92.

Bo faces the press one last time when he leaves the Tigers in August 1992.

Bo's Career Record

Year	School	W	L	T
1963	Miami (Ohio)	5	3	2
1964	Miami (Ohio)	6	3	1
1965	Miami (Ohio)	7	3	0
1966	Miami (Ohio)	9	1	0
1967	Miami (Ohio)	6	4	0
1968	Miami (Ohio)	7	3	0
1969	Michigan	8	3	0
1970	Michigan	9	1	0
1971	Michigan	11	1	0
1972	Michigan	10	1	0
1973	Michigan	10	0	1
1974	Michigan	10	1	0
1975	Michigan	8	2	2
1976	Michigan	10	2	0
1977	Michigan	10	2	0
1978	Michigan	10	2	0
1979	Michigan	8	4	0
1980	Michigan	10	2	0
1981	Michigan	9	3	0
1982	Michigan	8	4	0
1983	Michigan	9	3	0
1984	Michigan	6	6	0
1985	Michigan	10	1	1
1986	Michigan	11	2	0
1987	Michigan	8	4	0
1988	Michigan	9	2	1
1989	Michigan	10	2	0
TOTAL		**234**	**65**	**8**